Introduction

Did you know...

...that the Hundred Years' War lasted 116 years?

...that chewing gum was accidently invented while again trying to create a new kind of rubber?

...that Google was almost called Backrub?

Actually, only two of those statements are true. Your job is to figure out which one is the fake!

Welcome to *Two Truths and a Tall Tale*. On every page you'll find three statements—two of them are true, and one... well, not so much. To figure out which one is false, you might use your superior knowledge. ("I thought William Fleer invented chewing gum.") You might just take a wild guess. ("I know, number 3!") Or you might ask someone for their advice or look up the answer somewhere.

And just a hint—don't always assume the most outlandish statement is the false one. Sometimes truth really *is* stranger than fiction.

There are a few ways to play *Two Truths and a Tall Tale*.

You can play by yourself—but no cheating!

You can also play in a group. Have someone read the

questions and let people take turns guessing which one is false. Who knows, they might actually know the answer right off.

Or make it a race. That's right—take out your phones or tablets and Google (or Backrub) the answers. Either way you and your soon-to-be well-informed friends will have a great time learning interesting facts like these:

> More people work in the Empire State Building than live in Iceland.
>
> Twinkies were named after a line of shoes.
>
> Massachusetts has its own state polka...

...or does it?

By the way, we're not going to tell you which one of the facts on this page is false. You'll need to check inside to find out for yourself. All the answers—and some fascinating trivia—are at the end of the book, starting on page 97. But don't peek until you try to figure them out for yourself. You might even feel your brain expanding as you play. So what are you waiting for? Turn the page and get at it. You're going to have a great time...and that's the truth!

TWO TRUTHS and a TALL TALE

Sandy Silverthorne

Cover by Bryce Williamson

Cover Image © Electric_Crayon / iStock

TWO TRUTHS AND A TALL TALE

Published by Harvest House Publishers
Eugene, Oregon 97402
www.harvesthousepublishers.com

ISBN 978-0-7369-6900-0 (pbk.)
ISBN 978-0-7369-6901-7 (eBook)

Printed in the United States of America

16 17 18 19 20 21 22 23 24 25 / BP-CD / 10 9 8 7 6 5 4 3 2 1

The Famous and Infamous

Which one of these statements is blatantly false?

1. Thomas Edison, the inventor of the electric lightbulb, was afraid of the dark.
2. Billy the Kid was not really a kid. He was 43 years old when he died in a gunfight.
3. President William H. Taft had a cow at the White House that provided milk for his family and guests.

2

Great Women in History

Interesting facts about some amazing ladies of the past.

1. Even though England's culture in the 1500s is called the Elizabethan Age, Queen Elizabeth I died before such creative artists as Shakespeare and Christopher Marlowe came on the scene.
2. It took more than 50 years for the work of Susan B. Anthony to bring about the Nineteenth Amendment, giving women the right to vote.
3. Running low on medical supplies at the Battle of Bull Run during the Civil War, Clara Barton placed an ad in the newspaper, asking for donations.

Amazing Technology

Which of these facts are true and which one has been... *ahem*... invented?

1. The first barcode to be scanned was on a pack of Wrigley's gum.
2. The electric chair was invented by a dentist.
3. Walt Disney developed the technology of videotape recording in the early 1930s.

Fun Food Facts, Part 1

Some delicious tidbits of trivia to whet your appetite.

1. PEZ, the name of the popular candy treat that comes in the cool character dispensers, is actually short for the German word for peppermint.
2. The founder of In-N-Out Burger and the founder of Shake Shack are second cousins.
3. A large serving of movie-theater popcorn has more calories than 5½ McDonald's cheeseburgers.

Fun Food Facts, Part 2

Delicious food facts to suit your taste.

1. Pound cake got its name in England, where it was developed, because the cake cost a pound to purchase.
2. The fortune cookie was invented in the United States, not in China.
3. The state vegetable of Oklahoma is the watermelon.

Fun Food Facts, Part 3

Just when you thought you knew everything there was to know about food…

1. Idahoans celebrate New Year's by dropping a big potato.
2. The oldest soft drink in the United States is Pepsi Cola.
3. A ripe cranberry will bounce like a tiny basketball.

TV or Not TV, Part 1

Which one of these techy facts isn't technically a fact?

1. The Academy Awards, or Oscars, were first televised on March 19, 1953.
2. More than 60 percent of American households watched the final episode of *M*A*S*H* in 1983.
3. Dwight Eisenhower was the first US president to appear on television.

8

TV or Not TV, Part 2

Here are some little-known tidbits—one untrue—about the magic of Hollywood.

1. Mayberry of *The Andy Griffith Show* doubled as downtown Chicago for the TV show *The Untouchables*.
2. The TV show *M*A*S*H* was filmed in Hollywood, but the original movie was filmed entirely in South Korea.
3. The castle from the 1967 movie *Camelot* was the same set used for the TV series *Kung Fu*.

Pop Culture

See how up-to-date you are with these questions. If you're in doubt, ask your kids.

1. Jay Leno left *The Tonight Show* for good on February 17, 2014. He began hosting in 1992.
2. One of the most popular movies in 2014 was *Heaven Is for Real*. In it, a young boy named Colton recounts his visit to heaven after dying in a hospital.
3. At the 2014 Billboard Awards, visual-effects technicians created a hologram so that Elvis Presley could perform "live" onstage.

Fun with Toys

Toys are fun, but these little-known facts about them make them even funner. (*Funner*?)

1. The teddy bear was named after President Theodore Roosevelt.
2. Barbie's real name is Barbara Anne Sanderson.
3. Slinky, the popular wire spring toy, was invented by accident.

Now let's see, we've got Tubby, Burpy, Hickey...

Disney Trivia

Guess which one of these little tidbits didn't come from the Magic Kingdom.

1. Some of the rejected names for Disney's seven dwarves were Tubby, Burpy, Hickey, Wheezy, and Awful.
2. There's a full-size basketball court under the Haunted Mansion in New Orleans Square in Disneyland.
3. Michelle Pfeiffer and comedian Steve Martin both worked at Disneyland.

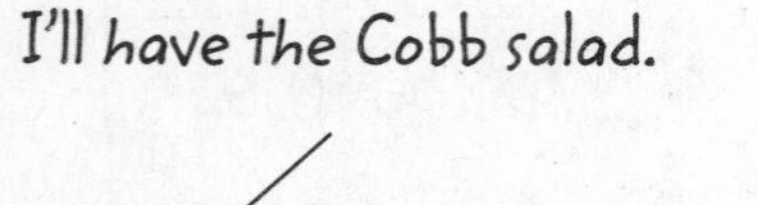

Food Creations, Part 1

Where in the world did these food names come from? (We made up one of these scenarios.)

1. The Cobb salad was named after baseball great Ty Cobb at one of his favorite Detroit eateries.
2. The popular Snickers candy bar was named after a horse.
3. Twinkies, the yellow sponge-cake treats, were named after Twinkle Toe Shoes.

13

Food Creations, Part 2

Interesting facts about where some of our favorite foods came from. And of course the obligatory lie.

1. The person who invented the orange powdered drink Tang also invented Cool Whip, quick-setting Jell-O, and Pop Rocks!
2. Popsicles were invented accidently by an 11-year-old who left his drink out in the cold overnight.
3. Cheese Puffs were created by a Costa Rican farmer in 1949 who had no idea how popular these little curls would become.

Food Creations, Part 3

You'll find these facts hard to believe. Good thing too—one of them is fake.

1. Astronaut Neil Armstrong was involved in the development of frozen TV dinners.
2. The Kellogg brothers created corn flakes while trying to invent granola.
3. German chocolate cake was actually named after Sam German and has nothing to do with the European country.

Fun Fast-Food Facts, Part 1

Hungry? Maybe some of these fast-food facts will satisfy your appetite for the truth.

1. There are more Burger King restaurants around the world than there are residents of Wyoming.
2. Dave Thomas, the founder of Wendy's, got his idea for his fast-food system while serving as a cook in the army.
3. Krispy Kreme doughnuts are kosher.

Fun Fast-Food Facts, Part 2

Which one of these interesting tidbits isn't really true?

1. The crossed palm trees at many In-N-Out Burger locations are a salute to one of founder Harry Snyder's favorite movies.
2. The iconic Big Boy statue outside of the Bob's Big Boy restaurant in Toluca Lake, California, was "borrowed" late one night in 1996 by two young but well-known actors.
3. Even though Krispy Kreme doughnuts have been around since the 1930s, their famous Hot Doughnuts sign didn't make its debut until 1992.

17

Entertainment Fun

Some amazing trivia straight out of Hollywood.

1. Kermit the Frog was named after creator Jim Henson's favorite childhood friend.
2. Steven Spielberg's first directing assignment was for a diaper commercial.
3. Oddjob in the James Bond thriller *Goldfinger* was an Olympic silver medalist.

18

Musical Notes

Some tidbits of info from the music world.

1. The creator of Fender guitars couldn't play one.
2. The idea for the boy band NSYNC came during a rehearsal for *The Mickey Mouse Club* TV show.
3. The Johnny Cash song "A Boy Named Sue" was written by children's author Shel Silverstein.

19

Amazing History, Part 1

Historical facts that may or may not be true.

1. Genghis Khan, the great military leader, was deathly afraid of water.
2. Leonardo da Vinci invented the helicopter, the parachute, and scuba gear.
3. Benjamin Franklin wanted the nation's official bird to be the turkey, not the bald eagle.

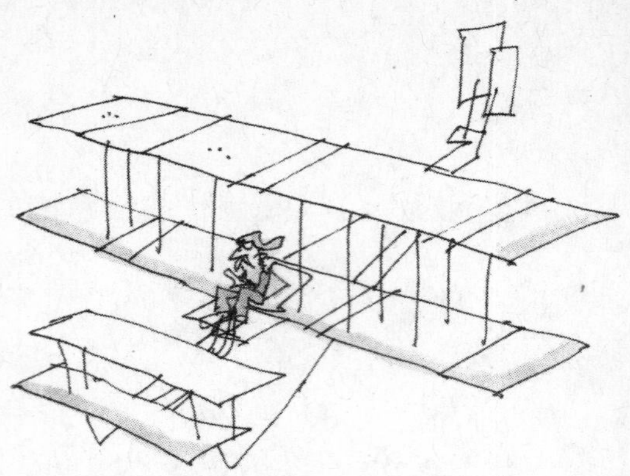

Amazing History, Part 2

Or not.

1. The *Titanic* was the very first ship to use the SOS message.
2. Thomas Jefferson was the first American to lose a presidential race.
3. The first airplane, flown on December 17, 1903, by the Wright brothers at Kitty Hawk, was named the *Wright Flyer I*.

21

Amazing History, Part 3

...that may or may not be true.

1. George Washington purchased Mount Vernon after the War of Independence with his earnings as an army general.
2. For many years, the man who came in second in the race for president of the United States became the vice president.
3. Washington actually fought for the British army for a time.

22

Amazing History, Part 4

See if you can spot the historical fake.

1. A 17-year-old designed the current United States flag as part of a class project.
2. Former president Herbert Hoover was Stanford's football manager before becoming president of the United States.
3. Supreme Court Justice Sandra Day O'Connor once worked as an assistant at a photography studio that specialized in pet portraits.

Movie Fun, Part 1

Here are some little-known facts (and one lie) that will make your moviegoing even more fun.

1. The longest film ever produced and shown was 85 hours long and was aptly titled *The Cure for Insomnia*.
2. Harrison Ford almost made it into the final cut of *E.T. the Extra-Terrestrial*, playing Elliott's school principal.
3. The same person who wrote Disney's *Finding Nemo* also wrote the script for the James Bond thriller *Skyfall*.

Movie Fun, Part 2

More trivia from the world of entertainment.

1. One of the names that was rejected for the novel *Gone with the Wind* was *Tomorrow Is Another Day*.
2. Humphrey Bogart never says "Play it again, Sam" in the classic movie *Casablanca*.
3. The envelope, please. The all-time leader in Academy Award nominations is Actress Meryl Streep.

State Beverages

Did you know that your state probably has a state beverage? Well, now you do.

1. The state beverage of Ohio is tomato juice.
2. New Hampshire's beverage is apple cider.
3. Idaho's state beverage is Yoo-hoo, the delicious chocolate drink.

26

Great Deletions

Which one of these "never once" tidbits isn't true?

1. Composer John Williams won an Oscar for best original score for the movie *Saving Private Ryan* but never once mentioned the director of the film, Steven Spielberg.
2. Sherlock Holmes never once said "Elementary, my dear Watson" in the Arthur Conan Doyle novels.
3. The biblical book of Esther never once mentions God.

Amazing Lasts

Here are the winners of last place in a variety of competitions.

1. In the Alaskan Iditarod dogsled race, the Red Lantern award goes to the last-place finisher.
2. Try as they may, Ohioans have never had a Miss America winner.
3. The last player picked in the National Football League draft each year is referred to as Mr. Irrelevant.

Totally Random, Part 1

Some interesting stuff that doesn't fit anywhere else.

1. A duel between three people is called a truel.
2. Fifteenth-century Chinese judges wore sunglasses in order to hide their facial expressions during court proceedings.
3. Baby beavers are called pups.

Totally Random, Part 2

Here are a couple of tidbits (and one tall tale) that will astound you.

1. The first selfie was taken in 1839.
2. Because of cats, the city bird of Madison, Wisconsin, is a plastic flamingo.
3. The city of Montrose, Colorado, didn't exist for 48 hours in 1967.

30

Totally Random, Part 3

See for yourself.

1. There's an airport in Sarasota, Florida, that will divert flights to other airports because of flamingos on the runway.
2. The winner of the marathon at the 1904 Summer Olympics actually hitched a car ride in the middle of the race.
3. In 2008 the Kansas State University Wind Erosion Lab was destroyed—by a tornado.

31

Totally Random, Part 4

Here are a few more really random bits of info.

1. During a three-hour baseball game, about one-third of that time involves action on the field.
2. The story of Rudolph the Red-Nosed Reindeer was created as a promotional item for a department store.
3. If you receive the Maurice Podoloff Trophy, you're the MVP of the National Basketball Association.

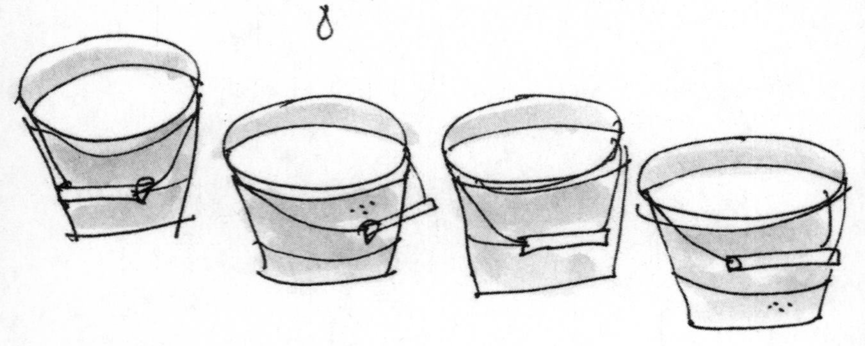

Who Said That? Part 1

Which one of these sayings is not based on a phrase from the Bible?

1. I escaped by the skin of my teeth.
2. God helps those who help themselves.
3. It's a drop in the bucket.

33

Who Said That? Part 2

Which of these famous quotes doesn't belong to the famous source?

1. Shakespeare made up the words "advertising," "assassination," "bump," "hint," and "lonely."
2. The phrase "broken heart" first appeared in the Bible.
3. Abigail Adams, wife of John Adams, coined the words "revolutionary" and "patriot."

Famous Dogs

These dogs were household names—or were they?

1. Former president Richard Nixon had a White House dog named Buster.
2. The dog in Dr. Seuss's classic *How the Grinch Stole Christmas* is named Max.
3. There were three Rin Tin Tins used in the 1950s television show *The Adventures of Rin Tin Tin*.

Interesting Jobs People Have

Employment facts from around the world.

1. McDonald's has 1.5 million employees worldwide—enough people to form their own country!
2. After the president, the highest-paid US government employee is the postmaster general.
3. More people work in the Empire State Building than live in Iceland.

36

You Can Choose Your Friends

Interesting info about some famous people and their families.

1. Until he became president, Harry Truman and his wife, Bess, had visited only three states.
2. Adolf Hitler's nephew once published an article titled "Why I Hate My Uncle."
3. Winston Churchill's mother was born in Brooklyn.

What's in a Name? Part 1

Can you figure out which one of these stories isn't real?

1. The original name for YouTube was 15 Minute Fame.
2. The ice-cream company name Häagen-Dazs doesn't mean anything in any language.
3. Google was almost called BackRub.

38

What's in a Name? Part 2

Around the world with interesting name facts and… you know.

1. Leonardo da Vinci isn't his full name. "Da Vinci" means "from Vinci," Leo's hometown.
2. Lexus automobiles were named after an engineer at Toyota.
3. The word *Volkswagen* is German for "peoples' car."

What's in a Name? Part 3

Even more fun with familiar names.

1. Pluto, now called a "dwarf planet," was named by an 11-year-old girl.
2. The term "London broil" refers to a method of cooking—not a cut of beef.
3. The name "hamburger" comes from the English Earl of Hamburger, the first person to come up with the idea of placing beef between two buns.

What's in a Name? Part 4

More name fun.

1. The 3M Company—manufacturer of Scotch Tape and Post-it Notes—is named after the initials of its three founders.
2. Starbucks, the mega coffee chain, was named after a character in the novel *Moby Dick*.
3. The athletic-shoe giant Reebok was named after a breed of African antelope.

Celebrity Names, Part 1

Which one of these real names isn't?

1. Rock Hudson's real name was Leroy Harold Scherer.
2. Whoopi Goldberg was born Caryn Elaine Johnson.
3. Keanu Reeves's real name is Jonathan Earl Gretsky.

Celebrity Names, Part 2

Here are a few more celebrities' real names. See if you can spot the fake.

1. Celine Dion's real name is Paulette Jean Mallory.
2. Charming movie star Cary Grant's real name was Archibald Leach.
3. Michael Keaton's real name is Michael Douglas.

43

Famous White House Pets

Which one of these presidential pets wasn't one?

1. William Henry Harrison had a goat in the White House during his time as president.
2. James Buchanan remodeled an entire room in the White House just to display his 1200-gallon tropical fish aquarium.
3. Herbert Hoover had two pet alligators that occasionally visited 1600 Pennsylvania Avenue.

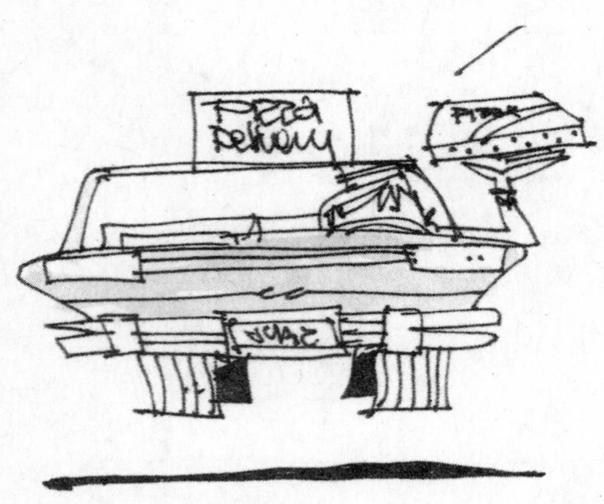

44

Pizza Madness

Interesting facts about everybody's favorite cheesy pie.

1. Approximately 50 percent of all pizzas ordered in the United States have pepperoni on them.
2. The word "pizza" comes from the Latin word *pissea*, which means flat or spread out.
3. Americans eat 350 slices of pizza per second, which adds up to about 100 acres of pizza consumed every day.

45

Cracker Jack Trivia

Some little-known facts about this sweet, crunchy snack.

1. Cracker Jack got its name when a salesman sampling the treat for the first time yelled "Crackerjack!" meaning that it was good.
2. The sailor and his little dog on the package are named Sailor Jack and Bingo.
3. The logo came into being before the molasses-covered popcorn and peanut treat was even created.

Sports Fun, Part 1

The NFL, the Super Bowl, horse racing... see if you know your stuff.

1. NFL quarterbacks have, on average, the longest careers in professional football.
2. The phrase "hands down" (as in, "She won the contest hands down") comes from horse racing.
3. The Cleveland Browns have neither played in nor hosted a Super Bowl.

Sports Fun, Part 2

We're just getting started. Guess which of these sports facts is a big whopper.

1. *Rocky III* was nominated for best foreign-language film in the 1983 Japanese Academy Awards.
2. A Major League Baseball player once got traded for himself.
3. Due to shortages of precious metals during World War II, the gold medals awarded at the 1940 Olympic Games were actually made of copper.

Here we go again.

48

Sports Fun, Part 3

What? You're still going? Well, let's see whether you can figure out which one of these sports tidbits is false.

1. The Rose Bowl is called "the granddaddy of them all," but the Cotton Bowl is actually older by one year.
2. John Kennedy, Gerald Ford, and Ronald Reagan have all appeared on the cover of *Sports Illustrated*.
3. In the early days of basketball, teams had a jump ball after every single basket.

Sports Fun, Part 4

Whew!

1. During one NFL season, the Pittsburgh Steelers and the Philadelphia Eagles combined to form one team—the Steagles.
2. To keep them from sticking to the ice, hockey pucks are warmed prior to each game.
3. Every single Major League baseball is rubbed in mud from a secret location before it's used in a game.

Animal Social Gatherings, Part 1

Try to figure out which group name is bogus.

1. A group of cows is called a flink.
2. A group of giraffes is called a shock.
3. A group of elephants is referred to as a parade.

51

Animal Social Gatherings, Part 2

Here are a few more animal groups with unusual names.

1. Owls gather in a parliament.
2. A gathering of eagles is called a convocation.
3. A group of pigs is referred to as a shimee.

52

Humble Beginnings

Can you spot which one of these rags-to-riches stories isn't real?

1. Paul McCartney of the Beatles and Wings was refused admittance to a music school in London because he "showed no promise."
2. Babe Ruth held the Major League record for the most strikeouts in a season.
3. Walt Disney was fired from a job because the boss felt he lacked creativity.

53

Bells Are Ringing

Or not. Here are two interesting facts and a fib about the Liberty Bell.

1. The Liberty Bell and Big Ben were cast by the same bell foundry, and both bells are cracked.
2. The word "Pennsylvania" is misspelled on the Liberty Bell.
3. The Liberty Bell was actually paid for out of the treasury of King George III of England.

This Great Country of Ours, Part 1

Fascinating trivia from coast to coast.

1. When the University of Nebraska Cornhuskers play football in their home stadium, the stadium becomes the state's third-largest city.
2. Did you know? At their nearest point at the Bering Strait, Russia and the United States are less than 250 yards apart.
3. The state of Louisiana was named after the French king Louis XIV.

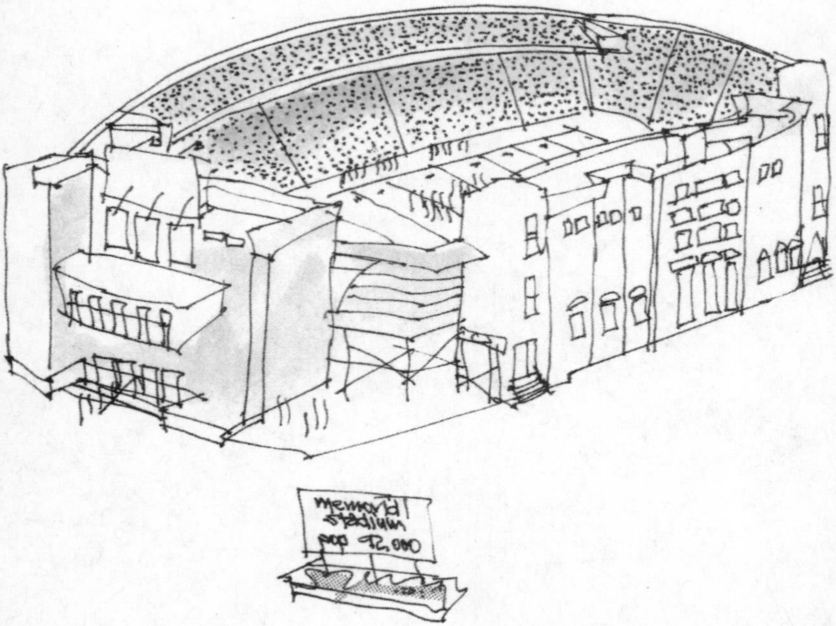

This Great Country of Ours, Part 2

Little-known facts (and a falsehood) about these United States.

1. Twenty-six states are listed on the Lincoln Memorial on the back of the five-dollar bill.
2. The most popular street name in the United States is Second Street.
3. Nevada has more national parks than any other state.

This Great Country of Ours, Part 3

Only in America.

1. Massachusetts has its own state polka.
2. Nebraska's state soft drink is Kool-Aid.
3. Arizona's state animal is the coyote.

This one goes out to Massachusetts.

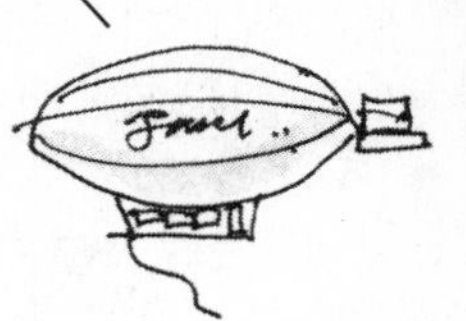

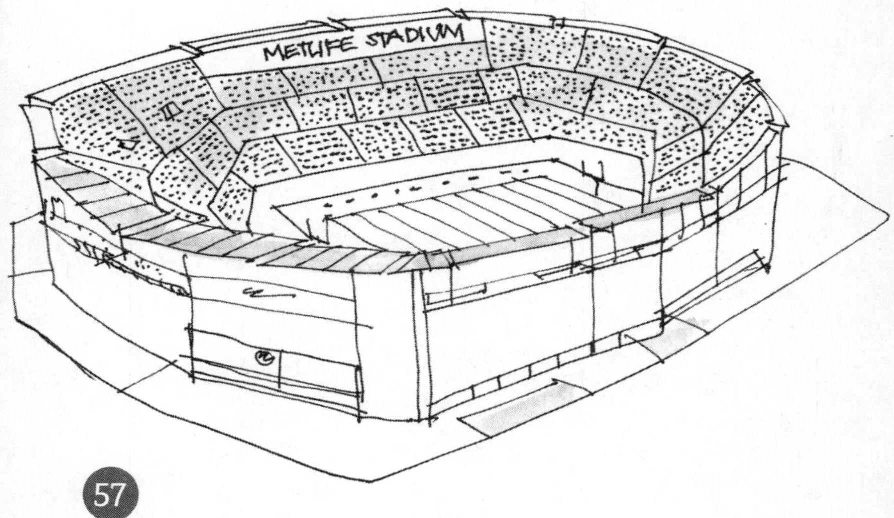

57

This Great Country of Ours, Part 4

Even more facts about these United States.

1. Chicago, Illinois, was actually located in Wisconsin until 1857.
2. The University of Minnesota is older than the state of Minnesota.
3. MetLife Stadium, home of the New York Giants and the New York Jets, isn't located in New York State.

58

Parade Fun, Part 1

Interesting facts about the country's most famous street processions.

1. In the 1930s, the giant character balloons from the Macy's Thanksgiving Day Parade were released at the end of the parade. Each had a return address label attached, and there was a reward for its safe return.
2. Kermit the Frog and Mickey Mouse have both been grand marshals of the Rose Parade, but Mr. Rogers never made the cut.
3. The first queen of the Tournament of Roses parade in Pasadena made her own gown and helped decorate her own float.

Parade Fun, Part 2

Here are a few more fun facts about everybody's favorite parades.

1. During a helium shortage in 1958, Macy's giant balloons were carried down Broadway on cranes.
2. The only person ever to be grand marshal of the Tournament of Roses parade more than once was Walt Disney.
3. Lions, tigers, and bears have been fun features of the Macy's Day Parade, but they were eventually banned because they scared the kids so much.

Invention Fun, Part 1

Check out these interesting facts about some inventions we all know and love.

1. Even though Alexander Graham Bell invented the telephone, he never once called his mother (or his wife) on his brand-new invention!
2. The refrigerator was invented by accident.
3. The first automatic dishwasher was invented in 1850.

61

Invention Fun, Part 2

Two of these are true, but we invented one.

1. The first president to have a phone installed in the White House was Rutherford B. Hayes. He used it to place a call to Alexander Graham Bell.
2. The first phone number of the White House was 1.
3. Even though there were very few phones in use at the time, Hayes had a direct line to his mother in Delaware, Ohio, and to the vice president.

Invention Fun, Part 3

Someone was thinking when they came up with these.

1. Olympic long-distance runners in Norway enjoy the benefit of having heated running shoes during their winter workouts.
2. United States astronauts have a patch of Velcro inside their helmets so they can scratch their noses.
3. Since 1945, all British tanks have included a tea-making apparatus.

Invention Fun, Part 4

A few amazing inventions that came about by accident—and one that didn't.

1. The microwave oven was invented by accident.
2. A lady named Ruth Graves Wakefield messed with a recipe and accidently came up with chocolate-chip cookies.
3. Doug Englebart's seven-year-old son came up with the idea of a computer mouse.

64

Invention Fun, Part 5

A few more amazing accidental inventions. Or not.

1. A New York chef created potato chips to satisfy a cranky customer.
2. Chewing gum was accidently discovered when William Fleer was trying to develop a new kind of rubber.
3. Ice-cream cones were invented when an ice-cream vendor ran out of cups.

65

Odd Laws, Part 1

Which one of these strange laws isn't really an actual law?

1. It's illegal to eat in a place that's on fire in Chicago.
2. In Maryland it's against the law to take a lion to the movies.
3. In Oklahoma it's illegal to wear a hat while operating a motor vehicle.

Odd Laws, Part 2

Stay away from these activities, or you may be looking at some hard time, mister.

1. It's illegal to serve a butter substitute to a prison inmate in Wisconsin.
2. In the state of South Dakota, it's illegal to fall asleep in a cheese factory.
3. In Oregon it's illegal to fish from the back of an open vehicle.

Odd Laws, Part 3

Silly laws that still exist in some states. And one that doesn't.

1. It's illegal to go barefoot after nine a.m. in Charleston, South Carolina.
2. In Iowa, tanning salons must post a warning about the risks of getting sunburned.
3. In Little Rock, Arkansas, dogs may not bark after six p.m.

Odd Laws, Part 4

More silly laws...or are they?

1. In Saint Louis, Missouri, a milkman may not run while on duty.
2. In Encinitas, California, it's illegal to apply sunscreen before swimming in the ocean.
3. In Mount Vernon, Iowa, you must obtain written permission from the city council before throwing bricks onto a highway.

Odd Laws, Part 5

Even more silly laws... and one big, fat phony.

1. You may not keep your horse in a bathtub in South Carolina.
2. It's illegal to lead your camel on the highway in Nevada.
3. In Rhode Island, you can get a ticket for carrying an open container of eggs in your car.

Rise and Shine, Part 1

Some breakfast-food trivia.

1. There was almost a fourth elf in the Rice Krispies family—Snap, Crackle, Pop…and Pow!
2. Cap'n Crunch's first name is Horatio.
3. Until 1978, Grape Nuts actually contained ground nut pieces.

71

Rise and Shine, Part 2

More interesting facts about the first meal of the day.

1. In Australia and New Zealand, Rice Krispies are called Rice Bubbles.
2. Basketball legend Shaquille O'Neal has appeared on more Wheaties boxes than any other athlete.
3. Frosted Flakes' Tony the Tiger was named after an advertising executive.

Animal Fun, Part 1

Quiz yourself and see how much you really know about our furry and finny friends.

1. Puppies don't learn to wag their tails until they're six weeks old.
2. One of the largest mammals on earth—the sperm whale—has one of the smallest brains. It's about the size of a softball.
3. Cats use their whiskers to measure whether a narrow space is wide enough for their body.

A Mob of Rhinos

Animal Fun, Part 2

More true and false info about animals.

1. Scotland's national animal is the unicorn.
2. A group of rhinos is called a mob.
3. All the swans in Great Britain are the property of Her Majesty the Queen.

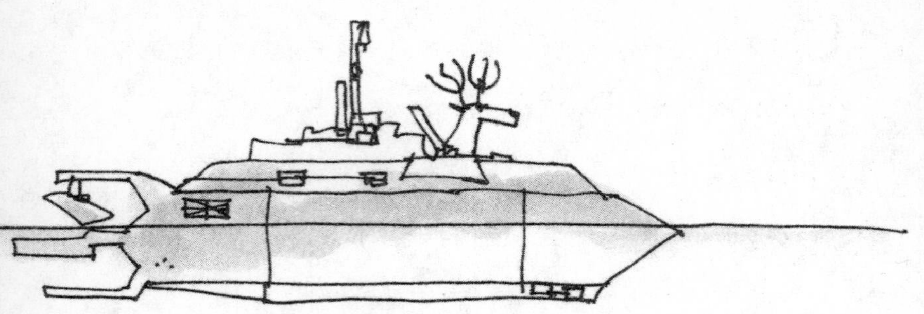

Animal Fun, Part 3

Here are some more amazing facts (maybe) about our furry and feathery friends.

1. Even though they're known as the king of beasts, fully grown lions are actually a lot smaller than fully grown tigers.
2. During World War II, a British submarine hosted a fully grown reindeer on board for several weeks.
3. In 1530 Spanish explorer Hernando de Soto introduced peacocks from the New World into Europe.

Animal Fun, Part 4

Which one of these wildlife facts isn't?

1. A group of rattlesnakes is called a rhumba.
2. If you're ever being chased by a tiger, jump in the nearest body of water. They are one of the few big cats that won't go near it.
3. Cheetahs are the largest member of the cat family to purr.

Animal Fun, Part 5

See if you can spot the fake hidden among these animal facts.

1. When baby giraffes are born, they're usually less than ten inches long and weigh between two and three pounds. In 1998 one mama giraffe in the Cleveland Zoo delivered four babies in a nine-hour period.
2. An albatross sleeps while it flies, sometimes traveling as fast as 25 miles an hour.
3. You thought *you* had trouble on your diet... a baby whale can gain up to 250 pounds in one day!

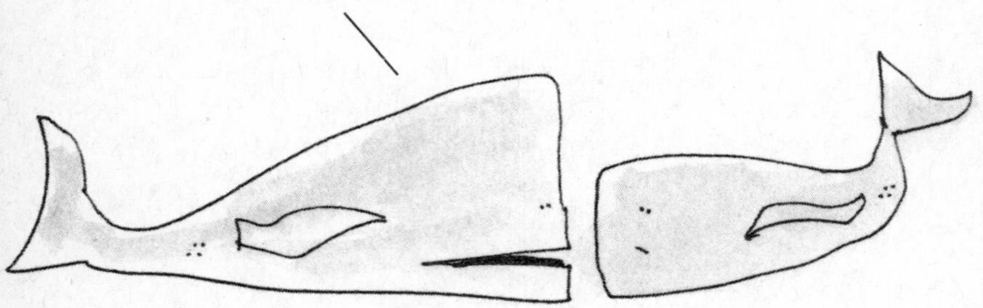

77

Animal Fun, Part 6

Try to figure out which one of these animal facts isn't true.

1. The band name Three Dog Night came from the number of dogs it takes to keep you warm on a cold night in Australia.
2. Turkeys were named after the country.
3. The first animal act ever to appear as entertainment can be traced back to Egypt in 451 BC.

78

Interesting Presidential Facts, Part 1

Our presidents are an interesting bunch. Can you figure out which one of these is not true?

1. Thomas Jefferson was the first president to visit the Alaskan Territory.
2. Richard Nixon once contacted the Miami Dolphins to suggest a play for the Super Bowl.
3. Ulysses S. Grant was once cited for speeding.

Interesting Presidential Facts, Part 2

Here are a couple doozies. And those are the real ones.

1. Herbert Hoover and his wife often spoke Chinese in the White House.
2. The "S" in Harry S. Truman doesn't stand for anything.
3. President Calvin Coolidge invented synthetic plastic.

Around the World, Part 1

Can you figure out whether 1, 2, or 3 is pulling your leg?

1. When the Brazilian Olympic team traveled to Los Angeles for the games in 1932, they came on a ship that sold coffee along the way to pay for their trip.
2. Las Vegas, Nevada, is farther west than Los Angeles, California.
3. The national anthem of Greece has 158 verses.

81

Around the World, Part 2

Interesting geographic truths (and an untruth) about this great big world of ours.

1. Bolivia exports more Brazil nuts than Brazil.
2. Duffel bags got their name from the town the material originally came from—Duffel, Belgium.
3. Lake Huron is the only one of the Great Lakes to touch five states.

Around the World, Part 3

More amazing world facts… and one untruth.

1. More people live in Durango, Colorado, than on the entire island of Barbados.
2. If you were to fly directly east from Hawaii, you'd end up close to Mexico City.
3. The population of Rome reached one million people in 5 BC.

83

Around the World, Part 4

We scoured the entire globe to come up with two nuggets. And made up the other one.

1. The Hundred Years' War lasted 116 years.
2. The Girl Scouts used to be called the American Girl Guides.
3. Butch Cassidy of outlaw fame was related to Albert Einstein of genius fame.

84

Around the World, Part 5

More amazing facts and a fib about the world we live in.

1. There's a theater in the Northeast where the audience sits in the United States and the performers onstage are in Canada.
2. Eighty percent of Missouri is actually higher in elevation than the entire state of Utah.
3. Until 1796, the state of Tennessee was known as Franklin.

85

Around the World, Part 6

More stuff from... you know.

1. There's a waterfall in Hawaii where the water goes up.
2. You can hike the world's smallest park in one step.
3. The number one export of Ecuador is aluminum.

86

Around the World, Part 7

More interesting facts (and a fable) from our world.

1. Former Russian president Mikhail Gorbachev once recorded an album of love songs.
2. Switzerland was one of the first nations to join the United Nations in 1945.
3. There's a city in Brazil whose name means "Don't touch me."

Around the World, Part 8

Some unforgettable facts about our planet.

1. New Zealand's 90 Mile Beach is actually 55 miles long.
2. In Arabic, the Sahara Desert is called the Desert Desert.
3. Saudi Arabia has the third-longest river in the world (after the Amazon and the Nile).

Around the World, Part 9

More little-known facts about this great big world of ours.

1. Scientists have been tracing the route of some lost rubber ducks for more than 20 years in a study of ocean currents.
2. Because of shifting sand, coral patterns, and volcanoes in the South Pacific, a new island comes into being every 72 hours.
3. There's a tall building in Japan where the tenant on floors 5 through 7 is a highway off-ramp.

Nancy Drew Whodunit, Part 1

Figure out which one of these titles is *not* a real Nancy Drew novel.

1. *The Scarlet Slipper Mystery*. Nancy meets two refugees from Centorvia who run a dancing school in River Heights. But soon she suspects that the two might be agents for the Centorvian government.
2. *The Secret of the Yellow Ocelot*. Nancy uncovers the clue to an ancient mystery when she discovers a missing statue in her grandmother's attic.
3. *Nancy's Mysterious Letter*. Nancy receives a letter from England meant for an heiress also named Nancy Drew.

90

Nancy Drew Whodunit, Part 2

Keep going—which one of these Nancy Drew titles is a fake?

1. *The Clue in the Old Stagecoach.* Nancy searches for an old stagecoach with a valuable clue inside.
2. *The Clue of the Dancing Puppet.* Nancy tries to unravel the mysterious performances of a life-size puppet at the old Van Pelt estate.
3. *The Mystery of the Howling Wolf.* Nancy and her friends experience mysterious occurrences during a camping trip to Coastal Falls Park.

91

Fearfully and Wonderfully Made, Part 1

Here are some tidbits about our amazing bodies.

1. You have the same "tongue print" as about 80,000 other people.
2. Every time you take a step, you're using up to 200 muscles.
3. Your heart isn't on the left side of your body. It's in the middle.

Fearfully and Wonderfully Made, Part 2

More amazing facts about these bodies of ours.

1. Our noses can remember more than 50,000 separate scents.
2. Adults have 60 more bones in their bodies than newborn babies have.
3. If you're trying to remember something, closing your eyes will help bring it to mind.

1. The Famous and Infamous

1. Number 1 is true. Edison was afraid of the dark. Perhaps that's what led him to create his most famous invention.
2. Did you choose 2? You're right! Billy the Kid was only 19 or 20 years old when he died in a gunfight with Sheriff Pat Garrett.
3. President Taft did indeed own a cow named Pauline that lived at the White House. As part of a cost-cutting program, Pauline provided milk for the residents.

2. Great Women in History

1. If you guessed number 1 was fake, good job! The good Queen had front-row seats for many of Shakespeare's and Marlowe's productions. Those guys were household names during much of her reign.
2. This is true! Susan B. Anthony began her campaign for women's suffrage (the right to vote) in about 1851. The Nineteenth Amendment was signed into law in 1920—14 years after her death.
3. Number 3 is true too. When Ms. Barton saw that medicine and supplies were running low, she cleverly used the press. She placed an ad asking for donations. She and her coworkers were overwhelmed by the response and received enough supplies to last until the end of the war.

3. Amazing Technology

1. It's true—the first barcode was scanned on a pack of Wrigley's gum on June 26, 1974. Now they're everywhere.
2. Yikes! This one is true too. Dr. Alfred Southwick invented the electrocution device in 1881. Apparently his dental practice was going through a slow time. You wouldn't want him to do your root canal.
3. If you chose number 3, good job! Even though Disney was a creative genius, TV wasn't even around much in the 1930s, so there would be no need for videotape. Besides, he was too busy producing *Snow White*.

4. Fun Food Facts, Part 1

1. This is true. PEZ is short for *Pfefferminz* (say that three times), which is German for peppermint.
2. Totally false. Harry Snyder (1913–1976) started In-N-Out Burger on the West Coast ten years before Danny Meyer was even born, and the two aren't related. Meyer started Shake Shack on the East Coast as a food cart in 2000. If you chose this one as being false, you're cookin'!
3. This is true too. A large popcorn at the theater also has more calories than four scrambled eggs, four strips of bacon, and four sausages. Think about that the next time you visit the cineplex.

5. Fun Food Facts, Part 2

1. Actually this isn't true. The term "pound cake" is from eighteenth-century Europe, where the recipe was created. It called for a pound of flour, a pound of sugar, a pound of eggs, and a pound of butter. (The original cake was more than twice the size of what we make now.)
2. The "Chinese" fortune cookie was created either at the Benkyodo bakery in San Francisco or at the Hong Kong Noodle Company in Los Angeles. But the point is, it was in the States, not in China.
3. This is true too. Weird but true. Oklahoma's state vegetable is the watermelon—a fruit.

6. Fun Food Facts, Part 3

1. This is a truism. Taking the lead from New York City, the people of Boise, Idaho, ring in the New Year not by dropping a giant crystal and glass ball but by dropping a big potato.
2. If you guessed number 2 was false, you know your sugary soft drinks! Believe it or not the first soft drink with a name was Dr. Pepper. It was created in 1885, a year before Coca Cola came on the scene. Pepsi came along in 1893. But generic root beer beat them all, being introduced in 1876.
3. This is true too. A ripe cranberry should bounce like a ball.

7. TV or Not TV, Part 1

1. This is true! The first televised Academy Awards show was in 1953. The ceremony was held at the RKO Pantages Theater in Hollywood, and Bob Hope was the host.
2. This is also true. Approximately 105.9 million people were tuned in to say farewell to Hawkeye, Hunnicutt, Winchester, Houlihan, Potter, Klinger, and the rest.
3. If you chose number 3, you win! The first US president to appear on television was Franklin Delano Roosevelt on April 30, 1939. He was speaking at the opening of the New York World's Fair.

8. TV or Not TV, Part 2

1. This is true! The Mayberry scenes were filmed during the day on the backlot at Desilu Studios in Culver City. At night, the *Untouchables* crew showed up and filmed gangsters running around downtown Chicago. Ah, the magic of Hollywood.
2. Not true! Both *M*A*S*H* productions—TV and movie—were filmed in and around Hollywood. The camp was actually at the Twentieth Century Fox Ranch in Malibu Canyon, just north of Los Angeles.
3. This is true too. The castle was constructed on the backlot of Warner Brothers Studios in Burbank for the movie *Camelot*, and it seemed like a good (and inexpensive) idea to use it for the *Kung Fu* series a few years later.

9. Pop Culture

1. Number 1 is true. Even though Jay left the show briefly in 2009, handing it over to Conan O'Brien, he came back. He finally gave up his seat for good in 2014.
2. This is true too. Colton was the name of the young boy in this "based on a true story" hit movie.
3. Actually, the visual-effects guys created a hologram featuring the late Michael Jackson for the 2014 Billboard Awards.

10. Fun with Toys

1. You probably knew this one. Teddy Roosevelt started the teddy bear craze when he refused to shoot a trapped bear during a hunting expedition. When word got out, newspaper cartoons ensued, and the toy teddy bear soon followed.
2. Barbie's real name is Barbara Millicent Roberts. She was named in a series of books published by Random House in the '60s. If you guessed number 2, you got it!
3. This is true. Mechanical engineer Richard James was working at his desk when he accidently knocked over some ship springs he was working on. They "walked" around the floor, and James was hooked. His wife came up with the name Slinky, and the rest is hours of fun history.

11. Disney Trivia

1. This is true! Good thing Walt and some of his artists got it together and settled on the current names. Let's see, there's Sleepy, Grumpy, Bashful, Doc…
2. A full-size basketball court under the Haunted Mansion? Don't be ridiculous. If you guessed number 2, good job! (The full-size basketball court is inside the Matterhorn, near Tomorrowland.)
3. It's true. Ms. Pfeiffer played Alice (from Wonderland) in the Main Street Electrical Parade, and Martin worked at the Cinderella Castle Magic Shop back in the day.

12. Food Creations, Part 1

1. If you guessed that Ty had nothing to do with the salad, you're batting a thousand. The Cobb salad was named after Bob Cobb, owner of the Brown Derby Restaurant in Hollywood during the '30s. According to legend, he created it in the kitchen late one night when he was hungry.
2. This is true. Frank Mars, the creator of the Snickers bar and head of Mars, Inc., named his new creation after one of his favorite horses.
3. This is also true. James A. Dewar, a baker and the inventor of Twinkies, saw a billboard for Twinkle Toe Shoes on his way to work one day, and snack food history was made!

13. Food Creations, Part 2

1. True! Sounds amazing, but William A. Mitchell, a food chemist for General Foods Corporation between 1941 and 1976, invented all of those cool treats and many more.
2. Truth is stranger than fiction. Eleven-year-old Frank Epperson from San Francisco left his powdered soda water out on the front porch during a frigid night with his stir stick still in it. Evidently the next morning he woke up and enjoyed the world's first Popsicle!
3. Cheese Puffs? In Costa Rica? Actually, these tasty little treats were created by American farmers Edward Wilson and Clarence Schwebke when they added cheese to their deep-fried puffs of corn.

14. Food Creations, Part 3

1. That sounds good, but number 1 is not true. Mr. Armstrong has many accomplishments to his credit, but developing frozen dinners isn't one of them.
2. This is actually true. The Kellogg brothers were trying to come up with a great-tasting granola but accidently flaked some wheat berry. So W.K. (one of the brothers) kept at it until he successfully created corn flakes.
3. It's a fact. German chocolate cake was named after American Sam German, the creator of a mild baking chocolate he made for Baker's Chocolate Company. They named his treat Baker's German's Sweet Chocolate Cake.

15. Fun Fast-Food Facts, Part 1

1. Nonsense! There are 544,000 people in Wyoming and only 13,000 Burger Kings around the world. Good guess.
2. Too true! Mr. Thomas served as a cook during the Korean War, and after serving more than 200 men a meal, he realized he could make the concept work in the marketplace.
3. Yes, Krispy Kreme doughnuts are kosher. The plant in Winston-Salem, North Carolina, where they mix all their ingredients, is certified kosher, and many of their stores are too.

16. Fun Fast-Food Facts, Part 2

1. This is true! One of Harry's favorite movies was Stanley Kramer's *It's a Mad, Mad, Mad, Mad World*, which featured a treasure buried under four crossed palm trees that looked like a *W*. Snyder used to say that his In-N-Out locations were his treasure.
2. Never happened. At least not to our knowledge. Young, well-known actors have done a lot of crazy things, but apparently stealing the Big Boy statue hasn't been one of them.
3. Believe it or not, Krispy Kreme's "Hot Doughnuts" sign hasn't been around all that long. Could have sworn we saw it during the Nixon administration.

ANSWERS

17. Entertainment Fun

1. This is true. Jim Henson grew up roaming his neighborhood of Leland, Mississippi—not with a frog, but with his best buddy, Kermit Scott.
2. Not true. If you guessed that number 2 was fake, you got it! Spielberg's first professional directing job was on a segment of the Rod Serling sci-fi TV show *Night Gallery*. Spielberg was 19 at the time.
3. Harold Sakata, who played the cold-blooded killer Oddjob in the 1964 Bond thriller *Goldfinger*, represented the United States in the 1948 London Olympics, where he earned a silver medal in weight lifting.

18. Musical Notes

1. It's true! Leo Fender, the engineer who came up with and developed the classic line of Fender guitars, never learned how to play one. He invited experienced musicians to test his new products.
2. If you chose number 2 as false, you win! We're not sure where the idea for this boy band came from. But did you know that NSYNC members Justin Timberlake and JC Chasez are both former Mouseketeers?
3. Number 3 is true. Mr. Silverstein broke away from his children's books just long enough to pen a smash hit record for Cash. "A Boy Named Sue" hit number 1 on the country charts and number 2 on the Billboard Top 10 during the summer of 1969.

19. Amazing History, Part 1

1. If you chose 1 as being fictional, you're right! We just made up all that stuff about him being afraid of water.
2. Mr. da Vinci did in fact invent all these things—and a great deal more.
3. Number 3 is also true, showing that even great leaders, such as Benjamin Franklin, can have an off day.

20. Amazing History, Part 2

1. If you guessed number 1 was false, you nailed it! A rumor is floating around about the *Titanic* being the first distressed ship to use the recently inaugurated SOS signal. But the truth is, another ship, the *Slavonia*, broadcast the signal in 1909—three years before the *Titanic* did.
2. Jefferson has the dubious distinction of being the first presidential loser. He ran against John Adams, who was elected the second US president. Previously, George Washington ran unopposed. After all, who's going to go up against the father of our country?
3. The *Wright Flyer I* was the Wright brothers' first flying machine. Apparently they were so busy figuring out all the aerodynamics, they didn't spend a whole lot of creative energy coming up with a cool name for their groundbreaking aircraft.

ANSWERS

21. Amazing History, Part 3

1. If you guessed number 1, you know your history! Washington never got paid for leading the Continental Army. Besides, he'd lived at Mount Vernon since 1761.
2. This is true! Until the Twelfth Amendment was passed in 1804, whoever received the second-most votes served as VP. Can't picture that happening now.
3. When the future president was a young man, he lived in a British colony. Washington served in the French and Indian War, fighting for His Majesty the King. Of England.

22. Amazing History, Part 4

1. This is true. In 1958, as Alaska and Hawaii were getting ready to join the republic, Robert G. Heft, a 17-year-old high school student, designed what was to be our new flag. (He basically figured out how to add two stars without making it too obvious.) He got a B-minus, but when his flag design was adopted by Congress, his grade was bumped up to an A.
2. True. Hoover learned some important leadership skills while managing the Stanford team in 1872—especially the day he forgot to bring the ball to the Stanford–Cal game.
3. Not true. If you figured out that Ms. O'Connor's life was a little too busy with her pre-law education to work in a "We'll Photograph Your Pet" studio, you were absolutely right!

23. Movie Fun, Part 1

1. Can you believe it? Eighty-five hours! It was screened from Saturday, January 31, to Tuesday, February 3, 1987, at the School of the Art Institute in Chicago. Wonder if anyone stayed awake for the whole thing.
2. This one's true too! Steven Spielberg cast Ford in the minor role as the school principal but cut the scene, figuring the movie star's appearance in the film would distract from the story.
3. If you guessed this was false, congratulations! Andrew Stanton wrote *Finding Nemo*, and Neil Purvis, Robert Wade, and John Logan wrote the Bond picture. Sounded pretty good though, didn't it?

24. Movie Fun, Part 2

1. It's true. The novel's brilliant author, Margaret Mitchell, apparently didn't have the same knack for titles. She also almost named Scarlett, Pansy. Whew.
2. This is true too! Bogart's character never utters these words. When Woody Allen wrote a play about Bogart called *Play It Again, Sam*, most people assumed the phrase was in the original.
3. If you guessed number 3 was false, you nailed it. Walt Disney has the most Academy Award nominations (59, with 22 wins). John Williams, composer of the music scores for *Jaws*, *Star Wars*, the Indiana Jones films, and many others, has 40 nominations and 5 wins. Streep has been nominated 19 times and has won 3 times.

25. State Beverages

1. Ohioans agree that tomato juice is their drink of choice.
2. This is also true. Residents of New Hampshire enjoy apple cider as their state drink.
3. Totally false. Although it would make a great choice, Yoo-hoo is not the state beverage of Idaho. In fact, Idaho doesn't currently have a state beverage. (Unasked-for fact: Most US states list milk as their state beverage.)

26. Great Deletions

1. If you picked number 1, congrats! It would have been pretty hard for Williams to mention Spielberg in his Oscar acceptance speech because he didn't actually win the award that year. *Titanic* won for best musical score.
2. Holmes said that iconic phrase in some movies and such but never in the original books. He did say "elementary" while speaking to Watson in the book *The Crooked Man*.
3. Number 3 is true too. You'll be hard-pressed to find any mention of God in the book of Esther, but His involvement in all the activities of the story is certainly implied.

27. Amazing Lasts

1. This one's true, friends. The Red Lantern award was initiated as a joke in 1953 but has come to represent perseverance and stick-to-itiveness. It is awarded to the last place finisher in the 1150-mile race. Mush!
2. There she isn't, Miss America… Not true! Ohio has won the acclaimed pageant six times! In fact, they join California and Oklahoma as the states with the most winners. Isn't she lovely, folks?
3. This is also true. Since 1976 the last guy picked during the football draft has earned this dubious nickname. But hey, many of them ended up starting for their teams, and some even made it to the Super Bowl. Take that!

28. Totally Random, Part 1

1. This is for real. It's called a truel. Seems odd though, having a duel with three people. Who's mad at whom? And what if two of them gang up on the other one? It's really confusing.
2. This sounds totally fake, but apparently these judges wanted to keep their game faces on so the defendants wouldn't know what they were thinking. (Can you believe they even had sunglasses in the fifteenth century?)
3. If you chose number 3, good guess! Baby beavers are called kits or kittens, not pups.

29. Totally Random, Part 2

1. The first selfie (actually, more of a self-portrait) was taken by Robert Cornelius in 1839. He had to sit perfectly still in front of his big box camera for more than three minutes to get the perfect shot.
2. Because of the cat problem and their propensity for catching birds, the good people of Madison opted to select the plastic flamingo as their city bird. Not sure if this helped the cat problem or not.
3. Number 3 is totally, 100 percent false. Sounded pretty good though, didn't it? But how does a city not exist for 48 hours? Guess we'll never know. If you picked number 3, good job!

30. Totally Random, Part 3

1. We're sorry your flight has been delayed because of flamingo activity... not true! Made it up. If you guessed number 1 was untrue, you were right!
2. This is true! The marathon course during the 1904 Olympics in Saint Louis, Missouri, was along hot, dusty roads, and more than half the runners dropped out of the race. However, American runner Fred Lorz hitched a ride in a car after mile nine and rode until the car broke down. He then got out and finished the race, coming in first.
3. Ironically enough, this one really happened. In 2008 a severe windstorm hit the Kansas State University campus and completely destroyed the Wind Erosion Lab. No one was injured.

31. Totally Random, Part 4

1. Not true! The actual time of action during a three-hour baseball game is closer to 18 minutes.
2. This is true! Everybody's favorite reindeer was created as a coloring book for Montgomery Ward during the 1939 Christmas season. It was written by a 34-year-old Ward's copywriter named Robert L. May. For a short time he considered Rollo and Reginald as his reindeer's name before settling on Rudolph.
3. The MVP trophy for the NBA is named after the first basketball commissioner, Maurice Podoloff, who served from 1946 to 1963.

32. Who Said That? Part 1

1. The phrase "skin of my teeth" is actually in the Bible! In Job chapter 19, verse 20, Job says, "I have escaped by the skin of my teeth," meaning he'd had a close call.
2. If you said number 2 is false, you're right! Even though it's often cited as being in Scripture, this phrase was made popular by Benjamin Franklin, the rascally early American patriot who gave us the phrase, "An apple a day keeps the doctor away."
3. "A drop in a bucket" is also in the Old Testament. In Isaiah chapter 40, verse 15, the writer says, "The nations are as a drop in a bucket, and are counted as the small dust on the scales."

33. Who Said That? Part 2

1. Can you believe it? The genius creator of *Hamlet*, *Othello*, and *King Lear* came up with all those words—and about 1000 more.
2. The words "broken heart" appear in Psalm 34, verse 18: "The Lord is near to those who have a broken heart."
3. So that leaves number 3. Abigail Adams, "revolutionary," "patriot"... we just made up the connection. She probably said those words. A lot. But they'd been around for a long time by then.

34. Famous Dogs

1. If you guessed that the thirty-seventh president's dog was not named Buster, you were right! His dog's name was Checkers.
2. Number 2 is true. Max is the faithful companion to Dr. Seuss's nasty main character in the Christmas classic.
3. This one's true too. One Rinny did tricks, another one simulated fighting, and another one ran with the horses in wide shots.

35. Interesting Jobs People Have

1. Number 1 is true! There are currently 1.5 million McDonald's workers around the world asking, "Would you like fries with that?" I'm not sure they'd want to be their own country though. Who would be their president, Ronald McDonald?
2. Number 2 is true too. Unfortunately for our vice president, he's beat out by the person who makes sure we get our mail in a timely fashion. The postmaster job currently pays around $276,800, and the vice president makes around $230,700. The president makes around $400,000.
3. Not true. Approximately 21,000 people work in the Empire State Building, and about 323,000 people live in Iceland. Hope you picked number 3!

36. You Can Choose Your Friends

1. Not true. Where do we come up with this stuff? If you chose number 1 as being the fake, good job!
2. This is true. Hitler's nephew wrote the article, and it was published in Germany before Hitler became chancellor. This same nephew later moved to the United States, joined the navy, and fought against his uncle!
3. Believe it or not, Churchill's mother was born in Brooklyn, New York. She later married Lord Randolph Churchill, whom she'd met at a sailing regatta, and took up residence in Great Britain.

37. What's in a Name? Part 1

1. If you guessed that 15 Minute Fame was fake, you're right. We just made it up. As far as we can tell it's always been YouTube.
2. It's true. The creamy and delicious "Danish" ice cream was actually created in Brooklyn, New York, by Reuben and Rose Mattus. They made up the name Häagen-Dazs to make their new ice-cream creation sound European.
3. This is true too. Founders Larry Page and Sergey Brin ran BackRub on Stanford servers for a year before registering Google.com as a domain. Whew—another name disaster averted.

38. What's in a Name? Part 2

1. This is one you can share. After all these years of thinking da Vinci was his last name, the truth is, Vinci was where the family lived. His full name was Leonardo di ser Piero da Vinci (Leonardo, son of Messer Piero, from Vinci). So there you have it.
2. Number 2 is false! Toyota named Lexus to mean Luxury EXport to the US.
3. *Volkswagen* does mean "peoples' car" in German. The familiar beetle design has been around since the late 1930s.

39. What's in a Name? Part 3

1. Believe it or not, an 11-year-old girl named Venetia Burney of Oxford, England, came up with the name for Planet X, as it was called before she suggested Pluto. She got the name from Greek mythology, which of course every 11-year-old was reading at the time.
2. This is also true. The phrase "London broil" comes from the method of cooking beef—first marinating it and then searing it in an oven broiler or outdoor grill. It is then served in thin slices. Yum. Some butchers will call certain kinds of beef London broil, but now you know the whole story.
3. Earl of Hamburger? We don't think so. The name "hamburger" comes from Hamburg, Germany, the small seaport village where sailors introduced the beefy treat. If you chose number 3, you're right!

40. What's in a Name? Part 4

1. You might have gotten this one right out of the chute. Actually, 3M stands for Minnesota Mining and Manufacturing Company. If you guessed number 1 was bogus, you got it!
2. It's true. Starbuck was the first mate on board the *Pequod,* the sailing ship in the classic Herman Melville book. Not sure if he was in charge of the coffee.
3. Number 3 is true too! A Rhebok is a type of African antelope known for its speed, grace,

and agility. Apparently the Reebok spelling was easier to pronounce—you know, no silent "H" and all that.

41. Celebrity Names, Part 1

1. This is the truth—Rock's real name was Leroy Harold Scherer. We'd probably change it to Rock Hudson too.
2. Somehow it's hard to picture Caryn Elaine Johnson starring in *The Color Purple* or *Sister Act*. Stick with Whoopi.
3. If you chose number 3, you got it right! Keanu Reeve's real name is... Keanu Reeves. Well, Keanu *Charles* Reeves. Good guess! By the way, "Keanu" means "a cool breeze over the mountains" in Hawaiian.

42. Celebrity Names, Part 2

1. If you chose number 1, congratulations! Celine Dion's real name is Celine Marie Claudette Dion. We figure she just shortened it a little to fit on the record labels. By the way, she was the youngest of 14 siblings.
2. Judy, Judy, Judy! Yes, Mr. Grant's real name was Archibald Leach. "Cary Grant" sounds more like a leading man, don't you think?
3. And yes, Michael Keaton's real name is the same as the other popular actor, Michael Douglas. According to Screen Actors Guild rules, no two actors can have exactly the same name, so out came Keaton.

43. Famous White House Pets

1. Even though Mr. Harrison served for only 32 days (he died in office), he did have a pet goat wandering the grounds during his brief tenure.
2. If you guessed number 2 was false, you got it! We just made up the 1200-gallon aquarium bit. Not sure whether President Buchanan even liked tropical fish.
3. The Hoovers were quite a fun couple. They did own two of these scaly pets during their time in the White House.

44. Pizza Madness

1. Number 1, your pizza is ready! This is true. Guess pepperoni tops (pardon the pun) all other choices as Americans' favorite.
2. Not true! Actually, the word "pizza" comes from the Latin word *picea,* which means the blackening of crust by fire.
3. We're not sure where these numbers come from, but apparently this is true. We Americans love our pizza—all 100 acres of it.

45. Cracker Jack Trivia

1. This is true. Cracker Jack's creators, F.W. Rueckheim and his brother Louis, gave a salesman a taste of their newly developed treat, and he jumped up and yelled, "Crackerjack!" a term meaning "Terrific!" The name stuck, and Cracker Jack was born.

2. This is true too. The Sailor is called Sailor Jack, and his little seafaring canine pal is Bingo.
3. The little Cracker Jack logo of a sailor and his dog was introduced in 1916—more than 20 years after the snack came into being. Number 3 is false!

46. Sports Fun, Part 1

1. If you said number 1 is false, you win! Quarterbacks are up there with an average career of 4.44 years, but punters and kickers—yeah, those guys who trot out on fourth and long or who try to put it through the uprights—actually have the longest average NFL careers at 4.87 years.
2. This is true! The phrase “hands down” comes from horse racing. When a jockey is way out in front, he can loosen up on the reins and keep his “hands down” as he and his horse head for the finish line.
3. Number 3 is true too. The Cleveland Browns have never made it to the big game, and they’ve also never hosted it! Maybe one of these days we’ll see it happen.

47. Sports Fun, Part 2

1. Yo, Adrian, this is true! The third installment of the popular Rocky saga was nominated for the Japanese Foreign Language Oscar in 1983 but lost out to *E.T. the Extraterrestrial*.
2. This is a great piece of sports trivia. It seems

that MLB catcher Harry Chiti was traded from Cleveland to the New York Mets for "a player to be named later." After a less-than-stellar 15 games with the Mets, guess who became that "named player" and went back to Cleveland? You got it. Welcome home, Harry.

3. False. There were no Olympic games in 1940 or 1944 because of World War II. And just for the record, Olympic gold medals haven't been solid gold since 1912.

48. Sports Fun, Part 3

1. Bet you spotted this one. There's a reason the Rose Bowl is called "the granddaddy of them all." It began in 1903, and the Cotton Bowl didn't come along until 1937.
2. Yes, these three presidents (and a few more) all appeared on *Sports Illustrated* covers. Kennedy appeared with Jackie in their boat, Reagan with championship athletes, and Ford by himself.
3. Talk about delay of game. (Oops, wrong sport.) It's true—until 1936, every time a basket was made, the game resumed with a jump ball. Nowadays the jump ball occurs at the beginning of the first half and overtime periods, and (in the NBA) after held balls and some other special situations.

49. Sports Fun, Part 4

1. It's true. It happened during World War II, when so many of the players were serving in the military that owners had to combine the two teams just to fill out the roster.
2. Not true. If you guessed number 2, you know your hockey. Actually, the reverse is true. Hockey pucks are frozen before the games to make sure they glide smoothly across the ice.
3. This one is true too. Every baseball that's used in a MLB game is rubbed in Lena Blackburne Baseball Rubbing Mud, a really fine mud found in a secret location in New Jersey. We know. We love our sports.

50. Animal Social Gatherings, Part 1

1. A group of 12 or more cows is referred to as a flink. A larger group is referred to as a herd. Or cattle.
2. A shock? Not true. A group of giraffes is referred to as a tower. Appropriate.
3. This is true. They might be referred to as a herd, but usually it's a parade of elephants. Even if there's no circus around.

51. Animal Social Gatherings, Part 2

1. We're not sure where this term came from (our guess is England), but it's true. Owls gather in a parliament.
2. A group of eagles is indeed called a convocation. Seems appropriate for such majestic birds.
3. A shimee? Really? If you thought shimee was bogus, you're right. Number 3 is false.

52. Humble Beginnings

1. This is false! If you guessed that number 1 isn't true, you got it. Sir Paul attended the Liverpool Institute for Boys as a teenager but never pursued any formal music education.
2. This is true! In 1923 Ruth struck out more than any other Major League player, but he made up for it by hitting more home runs than anybody else.
3. This is true too. The 22-year-old Disney was fired from an Indiana newspaper because he wasn't creative enough. Wow.

53. Bells Are Ringing

1. This is for real. The same English foundry that cast the Liberty Bell in 1752 also cast the Big Ben in London in 1858. The Liberty Bell was damaged during its trip to the United States and cracked when it was rung shortly after its arrival. Big Ben cracked because its hammer was too heavy.

2. Number 2 is true too. Evidently the employees at the bell foundry, in addition to making easily cracked bells, didn't have proofreaders to check little things like the spelling of the state where the bell was going to hang for hundreds of years. It was spelled Pensylvania. (Full disclosure—that spelling was acceptable at the time.)
3. This isn't true at all. The Pennsylvania Assembly ordered and paid for the bell. (By the way, it wasn't referred to as the Liberty Bell until around 1830.)

54. This Great Country of Ours, Part 1

1. This is true! Memorial Stadium seats around 90,000. Nebraska's largest cities are Omaha (409,000), Lincoln (258,000), and Bellevue (50,000).
2. We couldn't fool you, Bering Strait fans. Russia and the United States are actually more than 55 miles from each other at their nearest point.
3. Number 3 is true too. René-Robert Cavelier, Sieur de La Salle (whew!) claimed the territory in the mid-seventeenth century and named it La Louisiane—the Land of Louis. Glad he didn't name it after himself.

55. This Great Country of Ours, Part 2

1. True. You're going to need a pretty strong magnifying glass to read them, but there they are, along the roof of the Memorial.

2. You'd think it would be First Street, but not so. Second Street is the most-used street name in the United States.
3. Not true. Alaska and California have the most national parks—eight—while Nevada has two. If you chose number 3, you win! You might celebrate by visiting a national park.

56. This Great Country of Ours, Part 3

1. This is real. Their state polka is the peppy "Say Hello to Someone in Massachusetts," always a crowd favorite.
2. This is also true. Nebraska is the state in which the powdery sweet drink was created, so in 1998 they voted to make Kool-Aid their state soft drink.
3. If you guessed number 3 as the fake, good job! Arizona's state animal is the ringtail, a cute little thing that looks like a cross between a fox and a cat. It's a member of the raccoon family, as you can tell by its ringed tail.

57. This Great Country of Ours, Part 4

1. That's entirely bogus. Chicago has always been in Illinois.
2. The university really does predate the state. The school was founded in 1851, and Minnesota became a state in 1858.
3. MetLife Stadium is actually located in New Jersey. Yes, all those Giants and Jets fans travel to another state to cheer on their home team.

58. Parade Fun, Part 1

1. It's true. Macy's released the balloons with a reward upon their return. When a couple of private pilots almost crashed trying to capture the balloons (and the reward) in 1933, the practice was discontinued.
2. If you guessed that number 2 was bogus, you got it! Mr. Rogers was the grand marshal of the parade in January 2003 along with TV personalities Art Linkletter and Bill Cosby. The theme of the parade that year was "Children's Dreams, Wishes, and Imagination."
3. Too true. Ah, the good old days. The first Rose Queen was a charming young lass named Hallie Woods. She not only sewed her own dress but also helped decorate the car she was to ride in. Way to go, Hallie! Don't these parades get more beautiful every year, Stephanie?

59. Parade Fun, Part 2

1. True. Evidently there was a shortage of helium that year, so big cranes transported the balloons over the parade route. Somehow not the same.
2. Not true! Walt appeared as grand marshal only once—in 1966. His nephew, Roy E. Disney, had the honor in 2000. By the way, several people, including Shirley Temple Black and Bob Hope, have been grand marshal more than once. Dr. Francis F. Rowland, one of the cofounders of the parade, held the honor seven times.
3. Stand back, kiddies! There were lions and tigers

and bears in the Macy's parade for a couple of years—1925 and 1926—but the idea was nixed after the terrified screams from the children echoed through the streets of Manhattan. Not exactly the mood you want for a parade. On Thanksgiving.

60. Invention Fun, Part 1

1. This is true. The reason is not that Alex was a thoughtless son and husband, but that both his mother and his wife were severely hearing impaired and never got the chance to enjoy his remarkable invention.
2. Not so! If you picked number 2, you spotted the phony! In fact, several researchers, including William Cullen, John Hadley, and even Benjamin Franklin, worked for years trying to develop artificial refrigeration for food and drink.
3. Unbelievable but true. The first dishwashing machine was invented by Joel Houghton in 1850. It didn't do much but splash water on the dishes, so a better, more reliable machine was created about 35 years later by Josephine Cochrane.

61. Invention Fun, Part 2

1. This is true! Hayes had the first White House phone installed on May 10, 1877. And the first phone call he made was to Bell, who was in a hotel room 13 miles away.

2. And why not? The first White House number was 1.
3. So that means number 3 must be false. When the White House phone was first installed, Hayes had a direct line to the Department of the Treasury. Evidently he still had to write letters to his dear old mom.

62. Invention Fun, Part 3

1. Not true. If there are such things as heated shoes, we couldn't find them, and apparently neither has the Norwegian Olympic long-distance team. Number 1 is bogus.
2. This is true. Some genius (probably a nose-scratching astronaut) suggested they put the Velcro inside the helmet to ease that nasty itch.
3. This is true too. After a devastating ambush on June 13, 1944, during a tea break, a tea-making apparatus was installed inside each British tank. Who said war needed to be uncivilized?

63. Invention Fun, Part 4

1. In 1946 scientist Percy Spencer was working on some radar equipment when he saw a melted chocolate bar on a nearby counter. "Wow," he thought, "if this thing can melt chocolate, it could make some awesome popcorn!" (or something like that). His first microwave oven was six feet tall and weighed about 750 pounds.
2. This is surely the happiest accident in the

history of baking. In 1938 Ruth Graves Wakefield, the owner of the Toll House Inn in Massachusetts, ran out of baking chocolate while she was making chocolate cookies. She tossed in several chocolate chips instead, and the Toll House cookie was born. Well done, Ruthie!

3. False. Doug Englebart came up with the idea for a computer mouse in 1961 without the help of a seven-year-old child. If you chose number 3, you got it!

64. Invention Fun, Part 5

1. This is true. In 1853, George Crum, a chef in New York, had a grumpy customer who kept complaining that Crum's fried potatoes were too soggy. Crum responded by slicing the potatoes so thin that when he fried them, they came out crispy.
2. This isn't true. By the time William Fleer was working on his bubble gum (which his company is still making), gum had been around for hundreds or even thousands of years.
3. This is true. At the 1904 Saint Louis World's Fair, an ice-cream vendor ran out of cups. Fortunately his booth was right next to Ernest Hamwi's crisp waffle stand. Hamwi saw the solution—roll the waffles and drop a scoop of ice cream inside. Voilà! Ice-cream cones!

ANSWERS

65. Odd Laws, Part 1

1. Believe it or not, this is true. This law still stands on the books in Chicago.
2. Sorry, Leo. If you live in Maryland, you have to leave your lion home when you go to the movies.
3. Number 3 isn't true. You can wear all the hats you want while motoring in Oklahoma. But you *can't* read a comic book while driving.

66. Odd Laws, Part 2

1. Talk about cruel and unusual punishment! Yes, it is illegal to serve a butter substitute in a Wisconsin prison.
2. Believe it or not, it is still illegal to lie down and fall asleep in a cheese factory in South Dakota. Please nap at home.
3. If you guessed that 3 was bogus, congratulations! It's completely legal to fish from the back of an open vehicle in Oregon. But good luck with that.

67. Odd Laws, Part 3

1. This is not only untrue, it's downright silly. Who would care what time you go barefoot? Number 1 is the fake! Good guess.
2. Iowans have a little bit of the obvious thing going for them. In case you climb into a tanning bed without having figured out you might get a sunburn, the law is there to make sure you know.

3. Number 3 is real too. So make sure you teach your little critters to tell time before they go outside to bark.

68. Odd Laws, Part 4

1. Hey, you in the white suit, slow down! It's true—in Saint Louis, a milkman isn't supposed to run while on duty. Do you suppose it scares the cows?
2. What? No sunscreen in the ocean? Not true. If you chose number 2, you know your California skin-protection laws.
3. Number 3 is true as well. Apparently the whole bricks-in-the-highway problem precipitated the passage of this necessary law.

69. Odd Laws, Part 5

1. Try to keep your pony out of the tub, will ya? Otherwise, according to this century-old law, you could be in real trouble. In fact, to be on the safe side, it's probably a good idea to keep your horse out of the bathroom altogether.
2. Yes, this is a real Nevada law. Best to keep your camel on the side roads and surface streets.
3. Rhode Island lawmakers aren't concerned about you driving around town with an open carton of eggs in your car. Number 3 is false! It's best to keep eggs in the fridge though.

70. Rise and Shine, Part 1

1. This is true! For a short while in the early '50s, the Kellogg Company brought on a space-age Krispy pal. His name was Pow—to show the explosive nutritional value of whole-grain rice.
2. This is true too. Developed in 1962 by Jay Ward Productions in Hollywood, the good Cap'n's full name is Captain Horatio Magellan Crunch.
3. Totally made up. Never at any time has Grape Nuts included grapes. Or nuts. They're made of wheat and barley.

71. Rise and Shine, Part 2

1. This is true. Guess it makes sense... little whole-grain rice droplets filled with air. Rice Bubbles.
2. Not true. The number one Wheaties star of all time is basketball legend Michael Jordan. He's graced the crunchy cereal box more than 90 times.
3. This is true. In 1951, Eugene Kolkey, a graphic artist for the Leo Burnett ad agency, sketched the original mascot for a contest, and it became the official tiger of Kellogg's Frosted Flakes. He named the tiger Tony after Leo Burnett adman Raymond Anthony Wells.

72. Animal Fun, Part 1

1. This is true! You probably think you've seen puppies wag their tails before six weeks, but they don't. Wagging their tails is a form of dogs' body language—they learn to do it to help them communicate.
2. Actually, the sperm whale's brain is one of the largest in the animal kingdom. It weighs about 17 pounds. Number 2 is false!
3. It's a fact—cats use their whiskers to (among other things) measure areas they'd love to explore.

73. Animal Fun, Part 2

1. It's true. Guess no one ever said that national animals have to be real.
2. If you guessed this was bogus, you got it right. A group of rhinos is called a crash. It's a mob of kangaroos.
3. This is true too. By royal decree—the Act of Swans in 1492—all the swans in England are the property of the Queen. And recently, Her Majesty even took part in the royal swan census, called the Upping of the Swans.

74. Animal Fun, Part 3

1. This is true! An adult lion might be 8 feet long and weigh about 420 pounds, but adult tigers can be up to 13 feet long and weigh about 670 pounds.
2. Believe it or not, this is true too. The crew of the British sub *HMS Trident* received the reindeer

as a gift from some Russian soldiers. Not wanting to offend their allies, the crew took the reindeer, nicknamed Pollyanna, on board for six weeks until they landed in Great Britain, where she was taken to a zoo. While on board she enjoyed sleeping under the captain's bed.

3. This isn't true. Peacocks had been around Europe long before de Soto headed out on his explorations. In fact, peacocks didn't make it to America until the 1800s.

75. Animal Fun, Part 4

1. Number 1 is absolutely true! A group of rattlesnakes apparently shares the same name as the popular dance step.
2. Please don't do this! Tigers love the water, and chances are they can swim faster than you. So the best idea is to stay away from those beautiful animals altogether.
3. Yes, cheetahs purr like nobody's business when they are happy.

76. Animal Fun, Part 5

1. That's a whopper. If you guessed number one is false, good job! Actually, newborn giraffes are six feet long and weigh between 150 and 200 pounds. And giraffe moms almost always have one baby (or calf) at a time—occasionally two.
2. An albatross actually does catch a nap as it flies. Scientists tell us the birds do this to keep safe from predators in the water. And they seem to

have an internal navigational tracking system that keeps them from crashing into islands or each other.

3. These tubby little whales can gain that much in one day. They need the weight in order to survive in the wild. Their main diet is mother's milk, which contains 35 to 50 percent milk fat. We usually drink 1 or 2 percent, so if you stay away from whale's milk and follow a sensible diet, you should be okay.

77. Animal Fun, Part 6

1. This is true. According to the story, band vocalist Danny Hutton's girlfriend was watching a documentary on the indigenous Australian people, and the phrase "three dog night" came up, describing a night so cold you needed three dogs in the bed to keep you warm.
2. Number 2 is true also. Turkeys have always been plentiful in America, and many were shipped back to England on ships run by merchants who did most of their business in the Mediterranean area around—you guessed it—Turkey. The merry folks in England thought the birds came from that area, and the name stuck.
3. Number 3 is totally false. An animal act in ancient Egypt? We don't think so—the Egyptians didn't go in for that sort of thing. If you chose number 3, you're right!

78. Interesting Presidential Facts, Part 1

1. Not true. The farthest west Jefferson ever got was Falling Springs Falls, Virginia. He did send Lewis and Clark out West though, and they made it all the way to Oregon.
2. This is true! A few days before the Dolphins appeared in Super Bowl VI, Mr. Nixon called Dolphins coach Don Shula to suggest a pass play to their number one receiver. The Dolphins lost the game 24-3.
3. This is true too! Ulysses apparently had a need for speed, and he was cited for racing his horse and buggy through the streets of Washington DC. The fine was $20.

79. Interesting Presidential Facts, Part 2

1. As newlyweds, President and Mrs. Hoover spent almost two years in Tianjin, China, working in the mining industry, and they became fluent in the language. Apparently they spoke it to each other later in the White House when they didn't want others to know what they were talking about.
2. This is remarkably true too! Truman's parents couldn't choose between his paternal grandfather, Anderson *Shipp* Truman, and his maternal grandfather, *Solomon* Young. So they just gave him the "S." (The "J" in Michael J. Fox doesn't stand for anything either.)
3. Coolidge? Synthetic plastic? Not true. Synthetic plastic—or Bakelite, as one of the early versions was called—was invented by Leo Baekeland in 1907. If you chose number 3 as fake, you win!

80. Around the World, Part 1

1. We know this sounds made-up, but it's actually true! The sale of the coffee paid the way for all the athletes to get to L.A.
2. If you guessed 2, you're right. Actually, Reno, Nevada, is farther west than Los Angeles, but Las Vegas isn't. Glad you didn't bet on this one.
3. Greece's national anthem really does have 158 verses. But they sing only the first 2 at sporting events. Good thing, or there would never *be* any sporting events.

81. Around the World, Part 2

1. Believe it or not, Bolivia is the world's largest exporter of Brazil nuts. Go figure.
2. This is a strange but true fact. Duffel is the small town in Belgium where the heavy-duty material for the original duffel bags came from. Manufacturers honored the city by naming the popular carryalls after it.
3. So that leaves number 3. If you thought this wasn't true, you were right! Lake Huron touches only Michigan and the Canadian province of Ontario. Lake Michigan touches four states—Wisconsin, Illinois, Indiana, and Michigan.

82. Around the World, Part 3

1. What? If you guessed this one was bogus, you're absolutely right! Barbados had 287,400 people in 2015, and Durango, Colorado, had around 18,000. So unless things have drastically changed since that time, number 1 is the fake.
2. This is one of those facts that makes you think, *Really?* It's true though. Check out a map—Hawaii is almost directly across from Mexico City. They're both near the twentieth parallel.
3. Rome's population really did hit a million around 5 BC. Guess people couldn't stay away from those cool gladiator fights and chariot races.

83. Around the World, Part 4

1. Guess they rounded down. The Hundred Years' War really did last 116 years, from 1337 to 1453, including some short truce periods.
2. The Girl Scouts started as the American Girl Guides, but the name was changed in 1913 after just one year of use. Girl Guide cookies? We don't think so.
3. Made it up. No connection between Butch and the guy who developed the theory of relativity. If you guessed number 3 was false, you're bordering on genius!

84. Around the World, Part 5

1. Remarkable but true! The Haskell Free Library and Opera House straddles the border of Stanstead, Quebec, and Derby Line, Vermont. So most of the audience is situated in Vermont, and the stage is in Quebec. Do the ushers issue passports to go backstage?
2. Eighty percent of Missouri? No way! This is completely false. The highest point in Missouri—Taum Sauk Mountain—is 1772 feet high, and Utah's average elevation is 6100 feet. So if you guessed number 2 was fake, you know your elevations!
3. This is true. In 1784 the good people of Tennessee... uh, Franklin... organized a state named after one of the great statesmen of our country, Benjamin Franklin. But neighboring South Carolina opposed the formation of a new state. ("What are we going to do with all these states? Before you know it there'll be 50 of the darn things!") In 1796 the state was admitted into the republic under its current name, Tennessee.

85. Around the World, Part 6

1. This is true! Because of the high winds at Waipuhia Falls in Oahu, the water from the waterfall often is blown up the rocks instead of down.
2. This is true too! Mill Ends Park in Portland, Oregon, is a circle about two feet wide. It's located downtown at the corner of SW Naito

Parkway and SW Taylor Street. It was founded in 1948 by local journalist Dick Fagan.

3. That would be Suriname, the small country on the northern coast of South America. Ecuador exports petroleum, bananas, and cut flowers but not aluminum. If you chose number 3, good job!

86. Around the World, Part 7

1. This is true! In 2009 Gorbachev recorded an album of love ballads titled *Songs for Raisa* (his deceased wife) as a fund-raiser for her charity.
2. Not true. The UN was formed in 1945, but Switzerland didn't join until September 10, 2002.
3. This is true too. In Brazil there's a city called Não-Me-Toque—"Don't touch me."

87. Around the World, Part 8

1. New Zealand's popular beach just got shorter. Apparently when settlers first arrived, they took three days to travel the beach on horseback. Since they believed that a horse covered 30 miles a day, they thought the beach must be 90 miles long. They hadn't taken into account the fact that horses move slower on sand, and they only traveled about 20 miles a day. But 90 Mile Beach sounds better than 55 Mile Beach, wouldn't you say?
2. This is true. "Sahara" means "desert" in Arabic, so in reality the Sahara Desert is called the Desert Desert.

3. Not so fast, river fans. Actually, Saudi Arabia is the largest country in the world with absolutely *no* rivers at all. Zero, zilch, nada. Number 3 is false!

88. Around the World, Part 9

1. This is true! Here's the story. In 1992 a crate of these squeaky yellow bath toys slipped off a container ship from Hong Kong. For the past 20 years, these little floating ambassadors have washed up on the beaches of Australia, South America, Hawaii, Alaska, and even Scotland! Their surprising route has completely altered the way oceanographers look at ocean currents.
2. This is bogus. There are shifting sands, coral patterns, and volcanoes in the South Pacific, but a new island every 72 hours? We don't think so.
3. This is true! The Gate Tower building in Osaka, Japan, was built right in the middle of an exit ramp off the Hanshin Expressway. The highway tunnel uses floors 5 through 7, and elevators in the side of the building go from floors 4 to 8, bypassing the off-ramp.

89. Nancy Drew Whodunit, Part 1

1. This is a real title, published in 1954 by Grosset & Dunlap.
2. We made this one up. If you guessed the *Ocelot* mystery was fake, good sleuthing!
3. This one is real too. Sounds like we made it up because it's a departure from the series' title

formula, but *Nancy's Mysterious Letter* came out in 1932.

90. Nancy Drew Whodunit, Part 2

1. This one is real. *The Clue in the Old Stagecoach* came out in 1960.
2. This one's real too! The puppet started dancing in the 1962 novel.
3. Number 3 is fake! Sounds pretty good though. *The Howling Wolf*... kind of catchy, don't you think?

91. Fearfully and Wonderfully Made, Part 1

1. Not so! Tongue prints are as unique to each of us as our fingerprints. So don't go stealing any valuable art with your tongue anytime soon. The cops will find you out for sure. Number 1 is false!
2. Number 2 is true. Your body uses more than 40 muscles just to lift your leg and start walking. Add to that your arms, neck, shoulders (and hands waving hello to a fellow walker), and pretty soon you're at 200. So get walking!
3. The Pledge of Allegiance notwithstanding, our hearts are located in the middle of our chests, not on the left side.

92. Fearfully and Wonderfully Made, Part 2

1. Yes, our noses (well, along with our brains) can recognize more than 50,000 unique scents. What is that familiar smell?
2. False! If you chose number 2, good job! The fact is, the reverse is true. Babies actually have 60 *more* bones in their tiny little bodies than adults have. That's because as we grow, several of our separate bones grow together and form larger bones.
3. This is true too. Researchers at the University of Surrey found that when subjects trying to remember certain details closed their eyes, they remembered 23 percent more effectively than the group who kept their eyes open. Try to remember that.

More Great Harvest House Books by Sandy Silverthorne...

One-Minute Mysteries and Brain Teasers
Mind-Boggling One-Minute Mysteries and Brain Teasers
Awesome Book of One-Minute Mysteries and Brain Teasers

You'll enjoy discovering the answers to—or being stumped by—these interactive mysteries. In brief paragraphs and black-and-white illustrations, Sandy Silverthorne and John Warner present 70 puzzles, each with a logical "aha" answer that requires thinking outside the box. Clues and answers are included in separate sections.

Amazing Tips to Make You Smarter

Loaded with fun, offbeat trivia and Sandy Silverthorne's hilarious cartoons, this book will make you smarter and much more fun to be around. Who wouldn't want to hear which two first-world countries haven't signed a treaty to end WWII or where the phrase "a blue moon" came from?